ROME IN ROME

"You look for Rome in Ror
but in Rome itself you do no

... what is Eternal has vanish
the transient remains and end

—*Quevado*

BILL KNOTT

release press

Some of these poems first appeared in *Field, Milk Quarterly, Oink, Out There, Some, Sun, & Unmuzzled Ox.*

Paintings on covers & within by Marjorie Portnow.
Titles in order of appearance:
    Pownal Valley
    White Creek, N.Y.
    Don Rainey's Hill
    Eagle Bridge, N.Y.
Courtesy Kornblee Gallery, N.Y.
eeva-inkeri, photographer

ISBN: 0-913722-07-3
Library of Congress Card Catalog Number: 75-44678

First Printing

Release Press
200 Carroll Street
Brooklyn, N.Y. 11231

CONTENTS

DEDICATION PAGE

*Jean
and
Tom
and
Rose
and
Simon
plus
thanks
to
Paul O
Carroll
and
The
Body
Politic
Poets*

THROWBACKS

I want to take your place in my life so
I lie in wait for you everywhere. Once I used
To lie down in the paths of steamrollers, my teardrops
Were photographed at the feet of glaciers
To prove if they were advancing or retreating
Like positions in a kama sutra: after the cold
Ironingboard passed over I was fed lingeringly
Thru typewriters. It was read then that the
E-pore is used most frequently by my skin,
Next came x, p, o . . .

I want you to take my place in my life so
I follow you everywhere. Once I used
To follow burglars around: waiting at the window till
They ransacked a house then fled, I'd enter
Run my hands thru its emptied drawers, degleamed
Jewelboxes, my sole thrill was to follow rub the feel
Of deceived receptacles, rifled purses.
I'd wait outside, then rush in, clambering like an adam's
    apple.

I want to take my place in your life so
I go with you everywhere. Once I used
To accompany myself, I had a passport to the xerox,
The unanimous aimed its initials at me on the run,
When I died my clones were laid out at the funeral
Beside me, then a heckler who's amnesiac, anybody, some
Forever stranger was blindfolded led to the coffins to
See if they could get the right I by feel but failed
And so their life was took in place, and so I took your life
As place, so I must now keep placing your life in take,

In sudden give and take:
I want you to take my place in your life. Please.

(BLUE)   (DAWN)

Your ravished revlons give first aid to my shadow
(My flog-clinging tongue cuts another notch into your dildo)
While at the fledgling
Nut and bolt horizon

(Which bare flutters a single inflamingo-
Signal to my wrists being sandpapered
By shh-covered mimes) sotto-grotto
Voices lade the gates

Of habitual genitals with a statue
Who slavers up and down your toes' heart-rash
The figleaf

It impregnated gives birth to a kissglaze child
As one holds up a negative to view eclipses through
Through my elong eyes I gaze at him

2

WE ARE HAPPY HERE AT JUNGLEROT CONVENT

I recline supine
Waiting for the incognito to hit
But first tell me are uh you from the sunlit
Or the moonlit side of that star so sole up there

The history of bathtubs enters my stirrups as
I correct the clock's pronunciation
Of my future-length moans and
Kiss the Pretender to my mirror his pawn paws like

Hide and seek paved apples "I . . .
Am blind inside your blow
—In your caress, I see"

Ultimate
Inmate
Command me to tongue the clits of mediums in trance whose
    tongues are coven to your ancient whip-eeries

TANKATOWN

This island has
Been discovered by a great explorer,
But fortunately,
News of the discovery
Has not reached here yet.

THE WITNESSING

love my entwicer behalfer
my only endorser
yr souped-up autograph once
vowed freedom lay
across some gawky seldom sea

where were we going and me too
why strive to discover awe's
unstruck shore a flick
of the pen assumes it takes over
that distantsome responsibility

yet waves there you swore
dash in as if recklessly signing
over their power of alias which
should've made me stop right
there should've made me take
an oath to surrender here in
vitation to the shmoyage

my child my sister my
co-signer my friend our
destination today I say is not exotic
not far but like to re-use that
power of attorney simile is
in another's hands

and arms da duh dum maybe
your's whoever reads this poem
yes won't you please be its witness
just write your name where
indicated sorry I'd do it myself
but can't figure out which of
this octopus's signatures
is the legal one so sorry what's

your excuse

GOLLY MOUNTAIN BLUES

Up on Golly Mountain all the lovers are parked
Wish we could be up there enjoying the dark
But you don't wanna I'm sorry I came along
Cause you won't stop the car all night long
    Hairpin turns up and down the mountainside
    Hairpin turns drivin like a suicide
    I know you ain't to blame but
    Our loves about to flame out
    Can't you smell the rubber burn
    As you keep riding them hairpin turns
When you told me you loved danger I said then I'm your guy
I been dangerous since I first learned to kiss
Let's go up on Golly and give it a try
But when I said I loved it I sure didn't mean this
    Hairpin turns up and down the mountainside
    Hairpin turns drivin like a suicide
    I can't remember your name but
    Our love's about to flame out
    Can't you smell the floorboards burn
    As you keep riding them hairpin turns
I heard about some funny ways that people get their kicks
From runnin round upon the town to getting hit with whips
But you take the cake my friend you're oddball number one
I admire your nerves but I got some curves where you could have
    more fun than these here
    Hairpin turns up and down the mountainside
    Hairpin turns drivin like a suicide
    I know you ain't to blame but
    Our love's about to flame out
    Can't you smell the seat of my bluejeans burn
    As you keep ridin them hairpin turns
Poor baby I know it ain't your fault it was your momma she
dropped you on your brake when you was born cause if you
don't know that lovin is the deadliest thrill there is you don't
know nothin I shoulda known somethin when you picked me
up in the movieshow way your wipeshield wiper kept getting
into my popcorn here let me take these hairpins outa my hair

and let it fall down into your lap don't that make you want to
love me and cuddle and lay your head on my soft, soft shoulder
. . . Soft Shoulder? Hey! Look out!
> Hairpin turns up and down the mountainside
> Hairpin turns drivin like a suicide
> It's a dirty shame but
> Our love's about to flame out
> Can't you smell my poor heart burn
> But just keep on riding them hairpin turns

Get your tongue off that gaspedal baby
You tryin to love this thing or drive it well then drive it drive it
Just cause *you* ain't got nothin to live for . . . come to think of it
I ain't got nothin neither
Hey you know somethin? I'm beginning to like it
> Hairpin turns up and down the mountainside
> Hairpin turns drivin like a suicide
> I know you ain't to blame but
> Our love's about to flame out
> Can't you smell the rubber burn
> As you keep riding them hairpin turns

FUNNY POEM

death loves rich people
more than us poor
coffin salesmen look down their sniffs
shoot their cuffs
at us

funeral directors obit pages priests
all want classy
can't afford
a headstone
a silk lining
daily lawn mowers flowers plus
catering service for the worms
they get mortally insulted

and you know it's funny
while I never
believed that stuff about god
loving
the poor so much
made so many

I never believed that stuff about god
but this
death preferring the rich thing you know
it's kind of funny but you know
I believe it
it makes sense

in fact
I think we
should start a movement
our slogan would be
GIVE DEATH WHAT IT WANTS

yes
let's lend it a helpin' hand
be neighborly
it makes sense
since what death seems to want is
the dead
i.e. the rich

P.S.

after the carnival
suddenly mysteriously burnt down
they stirred the fortuneteller's ashes but
nothing will be found
to cast yr past with sez here on the fortune
card got this morn when
stepped up on the TV to see
what channel I
weigh

oh
no deep divining of death's lost
tealeaf left when
my cup cracks I wonder
cause the wind maybe

that blows away all trace of
livid stinging mote
right in your eye you'll
blink and blink be as
momentarily or eternally blinded as
sandhogs who come blasting stumbling

out of the sphinx's left
ribcage at dawn they
lost their way apparently

you too
with me caught in your eye will surely stray bump
into things that's
my big prophecy for today plus

in the arid plains of a
saladbowl the smashed broken
apart hooves of a horse
will be glued back together
with glue that's manufactured

from horses' hooves

UNDER/STUDY

an opera slept and
dreamed of its favorite diva
who strange was missing from
the dream

the buxom one the
pouter
breasted her upper
range runs scales beyond
the mere
maternal

have a chair
be hung by a hair
from the ceiling now
that's how to miss a high
c

ellipsical advice rose like decolletage
from its audience up to the muted
mastoided
opera

by now
just snoring fondish and low
like a decap
itated hairdryer

the audience sniffed
miffed
left

they milled outside in apartment
size groups or friends then
for one bosom moment merged then
fled
pelted by sculptors' raisins

their way of running the
scales maybe anyway one
of them
was left behind
as stand-in perhaps
as sacrifice

I stood there
flatchested aria
breathless solo with
a scales
nailed to my nipples

mistakenly begging each
bypasserby
to put all their tragedy
on one pan

comedy
on the other

POEM

As sexers sing thigh
   -low, -high
thigh
      low
          high
the hero manicurist with hammer and nails ready circles
seances like a key
spinning under the welcome mat on a desert island — the heiro
poet throws dice as he masturbates
and came snake eyes
                    I saw myself
riding in the car with my sexer and I asked him to step on the
      glue
I told him I was having problems with my anonymous
and he said that when Pontius Pilate washed his hands in DDT
his 20 queens were out sewing kneepatches onto Boot Hill — oh,

Truly I recognize myself:

as we hug in a growling sweaty love
like Goethe in Rome my darling thumthumms on my back —
counting off the seconds till the bank blows up

Flags that drape the coffins of assassins I salute them with my
      whip
each dawn — toe-graphology glided back and forth in its cage

— till halo leer gathers every stadium's broken home —

I am not talking to you but to
the plagiarist crouching inside my hors d'oeuvre

POEM WRITTEN TO A POET

bumpy kisses in the back
seat of a fast taxi soon
we're begging the driver to
hit every pothole in the road

when we hit a bad one suddenly
everything gets flung up hard
but fear is sweet on the
street of heart to throat

kisses usually get their kicks
from boredom the routine
tongues putting the proper punctuation in
that's why I like these ones

the middle of our poems too with
no warning a word jounces up
we write it down sometimes
fast as taxis doorstep us

then past our first date or
last it lingers though we try
we really try to let it be
just the split second it's meant to

SUDDEN DEATH STRIKES JET SET

well Peter Revson's luck ran out today
the Rev revved up once too
often

despite his rugged
good looks heir
to a cosmetics
fortune he

was driven
daredevil
death defy once
before a big race
his mother told him
he was crazy

Rev
age 35
one year older than me
a playboy
millionaire frequently
seen with the world's most
beautiful
and glamorous
personalities all

during his
150 thousand
dollar racecar nascar burning
crash Miss
World the fiancee was photographed
repeatedly

seconds after
the fireball burst his friends took
their friends aside
brusque to confide

15

that most eligible
bachelor of
them all is a mess

hell
he was positive
meteoric
to say the least

but don't worry the
whole thing
will be hushed up

a quickly announced
memorial foundation of
lipstick
nailpolish
nailpolish remover
eyeliner powder
puffs and pomades
proved useless
when applied to the burnt pan
cake skin

in
New York
Lauren Hutton is reported
to be devastated on
behalf of VIP's
everywhere thank you

one year older than me
hmm
say why am I writing this poem
is it to gloat
glad he's dead

16

glad I don't have try to be
him anymore a poet
penniless frequently
seen with the world's most
ugly and worthless
nobodies

and that's just what
I have to put
Pete down for
in the end
snobbery

even his pigheaded death
wish was a kind
of social
climbing I bet
he thinks he made it
today
into the not set

fat
chance
capitalist
rat

POEM

Alm for that saint who hung themself
With a noose tied to own halo
Alm their deaththroes toes shot out trans-
Pierce beyond ballet let us dance
Point, with a duncecap on each foot

Alm, alm our lack of mermaid tears
Must never weep or tears rust
Erode their scaley belows victims of
Self's salt tho impervious to sea's

Then alm our lack of ought other's each
Alm these arrows that have bandages
Instead of feathers at their ends
Alm for me away from you, far
Alm me away, alm for me:
Anemone me in your arms fresh
Like a laboratory sniffed by Tibet

EVOLUTION R

Sentenced to 12 whiffs of the pope
I protest
With curly hair
Or straight hair that grows out of the scalp
Then grows into the shoulders
Making it painful to turn my head
But thereby forcing a purer sense of profile on
A clearer renunciation of
Looking at what is called left right
But is never called
Asleep or waking up yawning
Breakfast an upper
Dissolved in turtlesoup
Waiter there's a hare in my slipstream
Hurrier all highs neutralize lows
Left right black white I try
Squeeze inbetween grey
Gray as sparks
Caused by rubbing obsidian ivory together
Dinner a downer going down on atalanta
Is this a race sniff sniff
Rabbit nosing turtle heels hold
The stopwatch on my dyings
Soon have them down to nothing flat
Faster than that even I'll go
Fast as a rumor of meat up
A soupline I'll flow
Rubbing rival chesspieces together
Is this my punishment
Looking neither left right
Panting straight ahead on course in a rut
But if so what was my crime
So heinous to deserve this what
Refusing to get my birth certificate
Punched at the proper intervals puberty
And gray hair or was it my crying
That the zoo has miscast its lead roles or
That heresy of trying to remain
My sperm's missing link sniff sniff
I protest

RACIST POEM

we had our chance Pilate
threw up his hands
left it up to us

we had our chance
we could have chosen
one of our own
a thief
a murderer

the cross the tomb the resurrection
then heaven
the right hand throne
a smirk on his face Barabbas
one of us

we could have chosen him
for son of god
might've stuck up for us up there
someone who was flesh
of our flesh

our kind
a pure one hundred
percent human
but we goofed

picked that halfbreed
that mulatto
from Nazareth

we had our chance Barabbas
a thief
a murderer
one of us

POEM

atlas hits me over the head
with a breakaway world
the atom bomb hitches a ride
stuck its thumb out his forehead

it's like ripping your fingernails off
drying them out
then carefully placing each nail
back on its healed over tip
just resting it there
no glue or anything
then trying to juggle them all in place
so good that the one you're with
can't tell anything's wrong

wait a minute atlas
baby I said
sure this is a rotten gig
holding up the world
but it could lead to something big

POEM

our prisoner has received a package
a cake
happy cliche
eagerly probes for
the proverbial hacksaw within

actually however
his salvation
his way out
has been carefully laid out
in
bright colored frosting over
darker frosting

the crucial message
the delicate pinkly lettering
overlooked
unheeded
falls shredded apart now
by his
hopeful search

INCH GIVER

pedantic chokeworms parsed
the last linkage of someone's blood
in the ditch

these split ditch decisions
exhaust me
their last sentence ran
thru a sewer

I had to find my way
what an excuse

that's why I lit that candle
destined to rip
the good samaritan's shadow
off its gutter

and what about those other candles I
saw once a whole
landslide lode of them each
was set upright
blazing
all of them tall upon
a long white dress's train
being drawn slowly
off over cobblebubble streets
it disappeared

deign-nodding
like a doublechinned
dowager
it went

the bumpy stones the stumble the
fall the smacking lips
what an excuse
last one in the sentence
is a rotten old period

ILLUSION

nowaminutes
more and more people are starting
to think
that they won't die in bed

of course
well that was always a luxury anyway
clean sheets
a starched nurse doctors whispering
doors shut quickly
to keep out drafts always
was a fantasy
a middle-class close-up
a big screen from reality

movie mythologizing's
where I learned
my favorite bit
of the legend
called dying-in-bed the
topsheet of course drawn
slowly up over yr face
symbolizing The End that
was my off

that really got me
steeped in
to my subconker
in fact
when I think of dying
now and then then
for a few seconds
I visualize it
happening
in winter

not in bed of course
that's not revolutionary-romantic enough
in the streets of course
and always
it's winter

winter what's
winter got to do with it
you ask

well it's silly
I visualize
I say winter in the hope that
don't laugh now
with the idea that
that the bloody
ragged shirt tossed over
my corpse
will somehow appear
to someone passing
on the other side of the road
at a glance
for a few seconds
might seem
as if it had been merely shrugged up
snuggled under
for warmth reasons not
that other

at a glance
for a few seconds
that's enough
for an illusion

HIGH WIND: TO MYSELF

Whoever heard of a cloud refusing passengers
—I reaffirm the virginity of all stigmata
By nailing your footsoles to mine and storming out to search
        for you
Palmists rub their genitals through your hands dowsers suck your
        tits phrenologists fingerfuck you

A smear test of my dreams reveals
That you are my friend long as you keep lettin the coffin
        bounce just once on your head
And you can trickshoot a penis right out of Buddha's lips
And your whip undresses itself on my skin

Flags slap the screeching sky awake but we we disappear
Upon whichever side of eyelid is the far
When yours carve this loftiness peer on the air

(Cloud like a banished pillow)
(Pillow that lovers keep adjusting beneath themselves to find)
(The right slant that of person walking against high wind)

You peruse my nipples with pliers
Extending the left one till it can flop over the right one
To suck Medusa's orange clit facelift
Which is painting your dynastic toenails
With tympani I burn with shame
To think I first heard your name whispered by aura-fetishists

PROCRUSTES' LULLABY

I have come to lay yr qualms
next to yr arms,
and yr arms alongside me.
I have come, are low confiding words.

Then gutter rolls,
vroom vestiges, clutch
ing down, my shoelaces tied to my fingers to remind me
to tie my shoes. You wore

a blue multineck threat, remember? torn
from off of the laocoonic figurehead the last
lava to slash over us bore on its prow but what's a newer
look in blindfolds this year, maim
manuals please copy. No no, the child!?

Quell
your fears, qualms lull, let arms fall.
Now go to sleep.

When you wake up we'll be there.
How many you ask?
Just the 2 of us,
give or take a few.

The superfluous parachutist
Wearing stilts so long they reach the ground and impale us
Lusts
To jump anyway

WEDNESDAY POEM

I place a boiling teakettle atop a dead volcano.
I crashdive a marquee, I claim it's
The sun glitters on this brittle sidewalk.
Then I run past whiffing the hair in my armpits.

You romeo manholes! I've just kissed someone
On her ear. Then, while puny puffs of steam
Rose from chipped obsidian, sipped daintily, carefully.
No sweat: her ear won't crack like a cup.

I walked her to her train; we said so long;
Her smile, her flash as the huffy train pulled away,
Like a knife withdrawing from robot flesh; sparks
From its wheels showered over me, black, lavacidal.

We'll meet 2 days from now: not enough time to enter
An anticipanthood, noviciate of rendezvous; to
Lift that barbarous cathedral, brush Samson's cindery
Dandruff off my collapsing shoulders, not enough time,

Nor space. Cramped. Thighs. She's travelling far
Away — I'm so foolish! Why did I propose dramamine
For fetuses when the trip from womb to world didn't make me
Sick—? Nothing makes me sick — besides, I like to walk.

2 days, 2 days. That's enough. I smile,
The sun kamikazes my footsteps home, past
The moviehouse, the grocery, candystore, recordstore, bar, the
Other places, wish there was enough room to put them all in.

SERIAL

my name is legion
was the favorite alias
given by fugitives enlisting
in the french foreign legion

my name is I forget but
I know whatever it is it's
the only alias
anonymous ever uses

REFLECTIONS

On my knees tickling a tombstone
with a knife: who does it hurt

is not the question. Nor, will we
cross the last hybrid together neither,

for emptiness to completely surround
me my object must cease, first. Last,

summation, oh, I could avoid you too
spoonfeeding my semen to a yoyo

fetus; wait, have we never met on
some ringside street or other, next

to some no-access parkinglot when
orange-bleak motordicks drag the lot

's wife across their open wounds, did
we kiss remember the hid lips

brushing bysworn cheeks with that same
air of exaggerated lightness, effort

lessness with which a conductor
first picks up their baton, or bus

token? could we exchange such simple
omens— Reflections off tombstones, globs

of earlobe jelly, that's it, that's
my object, my cease: did I stand, part, my

nostrils charmingly dilated and
ready to quiver a little, like a

startled swisscheese or did I fall
wrought-own these knees, slicing, pruning

all lost mirrors down to me's most
glimpsical, most you. Who

GERARD POEM

I lie face to face
with yr reflection.
Will moonlit lashes continue
to surround sunlit eyes?

I like to look at my reflection
in the dull gold of
the massive frames that
hold erotic paintings.

May I weigh yr palms
on the scales
of yr hands? Let's

synchronize our dimples then
fly off but not without
begging back down to them please
please remove all

consonants from star-maps?

2 BUTTERFLY POEMS

Clarinet

It's like a scissors
popsicle I don't know to
whether jump back
or lick.

Moi

A landslide
will get out of the way
of an avalanche.

AUTHOR! AUTRE!

My mother bore me to praise herself
Not that I might live
I praise her with fat fledgling palms
I build our nest out of compass needles
Am nailed to a false north
Pole where radar beams from hostile lands meet they
Huzzaw hiss embrace my voice-soluble alias of
Emergency broadcast systems deceased a
Minute of silence please if this
Were a real emergency I would applaud inadvertently
Clapping my buttonaire off
My nipples off
My bellybutton off
My hands would slam together with such erring force 'd
Knock off the eyebrow the ball my
Saint christopher bone and my breath
Soon
Nothing would be left until with much booing and scraping
Many-deign-on thanks to the grace of the generosity of anton
Antonich pavlov applause bares its ears and
I am born

ELECTROSHOCK IN THE ALMS POSITION

Who lives on the ground their nose gets raped by snails
And who lives at home the same thing fortunately
Lucky as the seventh abortion of a seventh abortion

I must continue my experiments Igor
Your breasts like spills wiped up immediately
Yes from my womb's leftovers raise the spurious youthwrath
     body

But first tidy up a mirror for my arrival stepping
From past or presto on to the naked thresh
Of its hold on my flesh just which one is it of

These pores that creaks when I pass thru dunno doorsill
Natal neon tattooing my illegitimate ghost on eel-tripled eyes
Thus sweat's features on stone memorized ambrosia's vomit
     faceless till

Yet despite this can you imagine it some messiahs still refuse to
Humiliate me in their dreams nevertheless I'll continue in the
     carpet
The little carpet-nails recite their lessons yet despite this the

Runaways' children will come home because because we need a
     sop
For poor prophets propped by pendulous navels a-
Board the meow express and the purr local where's that
     ingredients list

One mirror up which Medusa keeps rolling Sisyphus hmm
Let us pause for a millisecond tadpole injection
Let us assume the fallen poses of leaders not doe jam you fool

Animals animals worms snails similies realer than
Me a mole burrowing thru smokerings collates these collected
     offlurks of
Faster than a greased skeleton oh vast impure vasectomy of graves

37

Oh thunder-jacketed night my throat is filled with stranglers
Who lives under the ground their nose gets whiffed by flowers
Flowers petals stamens all kinds of flower stuff

For example I cram forgetmenots in my mouth wad
And chew and cram and chew till your memory
Drools out emptily slobbers down and stains me forever

(POEM)

like a room
high up
whose windows are in
have been carpentered into
the singular
diverse shapes
of
the loveliest object
each over
looks a room
would have to
ratio all window in that case
in that frame of things

thus and all
your cameo-clawed
face could reveal
carved
in forms of their
favorite views
its eyes for so
to see no be

oh
loveliest 2
singular 3
60 of the eyes
high up
or
even below the ground down there

a room

and

room

ORAL POETRY IS DEAD (IT TASTED LIKE THE WHIP'S SHADOW)

She made me dye her white pubic hair back
To its original black then had me lick it till it was white again
And in the distance the night like a whip's shadow
Came and went

It's enough to transmogrify your mogrifies
Her iso-splendor of arm pointed out
The last thought of Rodin's Thinker hovering around up there
In star-douche

O fires and semaphoric perversions
Dawn dild on my gildmold lids
Till they cover dice not eyes

(In the distance the singing of a sweat-shanty)
(Came and went as she kissed me)
(On the scars of open sesame)

While orbiting the earth
At a height of one inch
I notice
It tickles

Another fun date for you and your guy is get bloodtests done, then go down to the Marriage License Bureau at City Hall. Get in line, get your application form, then sit at one of the nearby tables with the other couples who are busy filling out their applications. Now comes the fun part of the date: looking at the parade of kooky couples who are getting hitched. They're unbelievable! Mismatched is no word for it: short ones with tall ones, fat ones with thin ones, old with young, all the weirdest combinations you could think of. It's the funniest show in town! When you and your date's sides ache from laughing and you're ready to go — pretend to have an argument. Scream louder and louder at each other till everyone in the whole Bureau room is looking at you. Then your guy should stand up, rip up his application-form, throw it down on the table, and run out "in a huff". Then you just throw your face down on the table and pretend to sob your heart out. Rejoin your beau outside, and you both can say you have had a really unique date. P.S.: this will also let *him* know where the Marriage Bureau is when the time comes for him to pop that certain question to you.

POEM DE PLUME

I hear a storm coming
faraway the thunder
sounds like a piece of chalk
dropped back in place
on a blackboard's sill
a tinny rumbling comes

if that's so
then it's just written
some word or name down on the night
a booming
hollow word for example windtunnel
an abandoned windtunnel that crumbles
retired astronauts loiter near it
like garbo-copped feels

no another word think of
a long reverberant word how about the
longest in our language attention-
span
which no one ever
reads all the way thru to n

n
maybe it's a name inscribed there on the sky
the storm's nom de plume
could be mine then
when your's if
we have a name one

one name not many
many as many
as a goose caught out in
the windstorm feels
signed stark
by all its feather-quills its
skkreak of delight
or pain

43

sounds like chalk on blackboard
faraway the thunder -
comes I hear a storm coming
to erase this poem

HOW DO YOUR FEET SLEEP SO BARE

Poetry is an act of creation
Alright but
If everything already exists in the world
Then all poems already exist
If that's so
Then
Since you can't create what already exists
In order to be a poet
A poet
Must choose the poem she wants to "create"
And then she must destroy everything
Including herself
Which is not that poem
Poetry is an act of destruction

HOMELAND (or: MY HOMELAND)

POLAND THRU THE CENTURIES a touring
Exhibition of maps drawn
By German and Russian cartographers reveals
There never was a Poland.

THE HEARTBEAT

A rollcall, droning on
and on, no longer heard,
forgotten. But what if one
time somebody yells "here"—

that would be scary.
As the death-rattle
at the end of a
tickertape, empty, that continues,
pale humming background sound.

But if any name
could bring response, out of all the
garbled list I'd guess her's:
it must have called "Anne" there
then, at last. I just hope I

was the one who answered.

—for Anne Ferrarese

47

ANIMA(L)

Her feet are bare sun
Milks sweat from as they pass
Should the evaporate pavements' scorch
To a cud-skeiny grass

The instant when the dew becomes penetrable
Quicker than them quote
Her strode presence's fading puddles
In this goad heat nope

Venus-proud feet up the sidewalk
Leave brief seas without a halt
And cowed I must follow to lick
Utter soleprints for my salt

—*for Carolyn Kizer*

48

MY MOTHER'S LIST OF NAMES

My mother's list of names today I take it in my hand
And I read the places she underlined William and Ann
The others are my brothers and my sisters I know
I'm going to see them when I'm fully grown

Yes they're waiting for me to join em and I will
Just over the top of that next big hill
Lies a green valley where their shouts of joy are fellowing
Save all but one can be seen there next a kin

And a link is missing from their ringarosey dance
Think of the names she wrote down not just by chance
When she learned that a baby inside her was growing small
She placed that list inside the family Bible

Then I was born and she died soon after
And I grew up sinful of questions I could not ask her
I did'not know that she had left me the answer
Pressed between the holy pages with the happy laughter
Of John, Rudolph, Frank, Arthur, Paul,
Pauline, Martha, Ann, Doris, Susan, you all,

I did not even know you were alive
Till I read the Bible today for the first time in my life
And I found this list of names that might have been my own
You other me's on the bright side of my moon

Mother and Daddy too have joined you in play
And I am coming to complete the circle of your day
I was a lonely child I never understood that you
Were waiting for me to find the truth and know

And I'll make this one promise you want me to:
I'm goin to continue my Bible study
Till I'm back inside the Body
With you

POEM

If I had a magic carpet I'd keep it
Floating always right in front of me
Perpendicular, like a door.
Open or closed? you ask,

Open to let us in then close of course.

WAR

a chickenleg discoursing in mid air
with paprika
the old argument
friends enemies cluster
around their mouths

that
is the symtomology of the dead
someone's fist proposes
the table hit on the head
repeatedly I get your point
Damocles said
playing mumbleypeg
with fleeing cockroaches

you don't understand
the whole world is at war
only we
are calm
and quarrelsome namely the
plates are whisked away
as though by magic
only we are real

a bottle
leveled off
razed off with the glasses the discussion
grinds lower
and lower
like the dumbwaiter
into bowels of silence

now
each one sprawls apart
swollen waiting
for the stuntmen
and the stuntwomen
to come caress them
with dogtags

GET IN LINE

surreptitious
and mute
as the vendors of my beauty it

usually takes take
place lost

usually

hide and seek
interceptors hucksters
toothpick
aristocrats

their fob off game
's a waste of time times
space loss

equals toss

of playing card
faces into a hat that's simultaneously
been tossed into a halo on
the fly so to speak

though I know
I'm supposed to say
on the wing

LOURDES

There are miracles that nobody survives
Observers of to remember where or when
And these are the only true miracles
Since we never hear about them

Since we never hear about them
It increases their chance of being common
Everyday things without witness without
Us even how absently close we brush

Teeth sneeze cook supper mail post
Cards in contrast official miracles take
A far off locale verifiable visitable
Some backwater never heard before of since

Not pop the map but part the pilgrim's lips it
Springs up hospitals hotdog stands pour in
Testeroniacs pimple victims even
For credentials cripples pour in

Their limbs hung all whichway on them
Signslats nailed on a slanting
Direction-post at a muddy crossroads
In the boondocks of a forgotten place

FELLATIO POEM

I go for oops on
the downy cymbals your
prune-
pure scrotum holds
apart, ready.

When
you come the clash
hyphenates
my ears.

BAKE-OFF

They wandered thru the hand in hand.
They found themselves winners of each other's
Look-alike contests, but weren't surprised?

Other strangers than our own may remember
Forget to lick the birthmarks off,
We . . . they joined hands with a wand.

Then, on a high ship's-prow, all took
Turns being the figurehead. An awkward
Straps contraption held each partner above the other,

Whose prey prevails sails these drain-edged seas.
We took turns, finally nobody wins,
Someone was ripping the figleaf off of Janus's
Face. At last, somebody cried.

Other strangers than our own may remember,
We . . . they . . .

WHOM

an hourglass must always be smashed
upon a sundial
I seem to remember
a weathervane's what you turn a churn
with right

oillamps tuck us in at night a thimble
is put for bait on a hook a book's
for boarding over
the moon a
handwritten letter what's that

all these useless objects
obsolete esthetic done for
are found in my poems
nevertheless

for though
a device a day is lost to the
sift of the antiqueshop
it's no go
the names remain
if not the function
history
as yet
has no successfully erased pages

I wonder why
maybe

down in a well
powered by a purist windmill
someone's diary of damocles hoards
all those blank pages

lost
and hiding down there
nevertheless

PASS THE PLASMA, PHANTASMA

Standing on the youthhold I saw a shooting star
And knew it predestined encounter with the sole love
But that comet crashed into the earth so hard
Tilted its axis a little bit not much just enough
So I will miss meeting her by a few yards

All through day you kept combing your hair
In directions of the light length of mane
Followed the sun all day and ended up hanging straight down
Over your right ear
Forgive me: I'd never done it that way before

Quevado wrote he would be dust but dust in love
And while I can't believe that millions from now
A quartzstone and a rose will embrace
I can believe still less that my arms are around you now, and that
Your sharp crystals are tearing my petals

Mathematically when it's 2
Lovers each halves their loneliness
With 4 in bed it's quartered
At an orgy loneliness must be a drop squeezed to the wall
Which it enters as pure alcohol

SUCCESS

First they cut a notch across my shins.
My thighs next received a slash . . . then belly, chest.
Higher and higher the gouges come.

How long till you get tall enough,
so it'll be my turn to be measured upon you—
no, this is not Procrustes' lullaby. It's petulance:

will we always be walls up which the scars of
successive childhoods climb — must we stand
flat against each other trembling, tiptoe, tense,

while some adult approaches with a knife in their hand?

PASSING

at the trackmeet to meet somebody I
don't know who suddenly
I find myself in the relay

around my baton the
finish-line string is tied
tight painful a reminder
of the terrifying
decision coming up

3 candidates
squeamishly await my hand-off
a centaur
a mermaid
and Lord Chatterly

who should I pass it on to
can any of them win which
lineage will I choose
which thread

rub cinders in my eyes
hang hurdles
round my neck I can't
make up my mind no
way

the irrevokable choice agonizes me
like a stitch in the side
the frightend crowd is cheering
I'm nearing the hand-on point still
uncertain
dizzy
desperate

then I get an idea
a familiar idea
in moments of crisis
and false starts what
if I just poof

I mean disappear
but so
purely so
explosively that

they'd
have to make everybody
in the whole rang stadium line
up for hours and
franticly search all
of them at the exits

frantic I say
but would they
find even
a trace of me
would this mean I've
successfully

or victoriously
one of them

completed the transference that
tortures me above

BREAKFAST

You know how I like my dawns god   'll
Just   tap   off   this   nubei-pink   'n'   'n'
Call yuh call
        That a 3 minute dawn?!!

You need a new timer old timer

UP TO NOW

That's how
an amputated juggler
—minus head arms legs—
kept on juggling.

He rolled thru the dust:
torso of scabs, half-dead lump
bounced dishes globes skies
off of himself, kept them
from falling smash until
somebody came by and
tossed him up too—
in homage—or carelessness—or lust.

That's how,
your heart kept beating
up to this moment.

RITUAL

first
bury your hands
then the third from the right toes
your pancreas bury it next
and so on in the order proscribed by ancient ires
save the head for last
cup your thumbs benearth for it to fall into
have an eyelash
be the last thing visible overground
leave a heartbeat
to tamp down the dirt
a blink
to be a shadow for grassblade above
then nothing up there
at the beginning of this poem nothing
so that the last the only
all that'll be left to do then is
bury your hands

Rome In Rome is printed in an edition of 2000, 26 of which have been lettered A-Z & signed by the author.